LETTERS TO A SON

Printed in the United States of America.

ISBN 978-0-9970242-4-1

J Winthrop, Charleston, South Carolina

www.winthropfamily.org

watercolor by Gwendolyn McGee

Edward Field Winthrop

To Libby
and
Ted's older brothers.

PRELUDE

There are famous literary precedents for *Letters to a Son*, notably Chesterfield in the eighteenth century – a work whose relation to the present volume is only a coincidence of title.

John Winthrop does not pontificate, he does not intellectualize. There is no attempt at Ciceronian rhetoric, no intent to speak to an audience larger than that of his gestating and ultimately newborn son. He writes from the heart and not the head.

The reader feels privileged to share a father's affection for his nascent child and enter into their special, private world.

For the very appeal of these letters is their total sincerity. In these mini-essays, several of which have already been published in the *Greenwich Times*, John Winthrop – my Harvard classmate and longtime friend – touches one of the great human cores, and puts onto paper words that most fathers find difficult to articulate. He has expressed feelings that are ineffable as well as universal.

John's sensitive brilliance is enhanced by the wonderful artwork of Gwendolyn McGee and the superior graphic design of John Davis.

We fathers thank you for this gift, John. We can now read aloud and emulate the special parent/child relationship you have so touchingly established.

Erich Segal

London
July, 1989

February 1986

Dear Son,

At 6:07 on this wintry morning I got out of bed to go for a walk. I was thinking that nobody knows your name yet; nobody knows where our family will live or how the world will change once you enter it. Through the miracle of modern science we do know that you are a boy and that you will be born about June 17th of this year. Your mother and I also know that we love you and that we will do our best to give you a spirited introduction to your journey through life.

In a while we will think more about your name but for now fixing up the house in preparation for your arrival seems more important. Within the past few days you have begun to roll and kick. So we know you are a reality and that we had better get ready for your arrival. Your date of birth is expected to be about a week before my fiftieth birthday, so I'll be a little old for you but I'll do my best to keep up.

Meanwhile, I'll try to write you letters from time to time. With luck, these letters will give you a picture of your parents, your family and the world you will be entering. At an early age you will develop your own ideas on all three subjects. At a minimum these few letters I write you in early childhood and beforehand will convey a rambling and irregular view of the world as I know it and, hopefully, they will provide continuity, provoke thought, or humour, or amusement in a world that needs all of the above.

Love,
Dad

June 28, 1986

Dear Ted,

Today at 1:03 in the morning you entered this world weighing 9 pounds, 11 ounces. You were patient and polite (like your mother), allowing your father and your eldest brother to celebrate their birthdays quietly on the 22nd and the 27th of June, respectively. On the other hand, you clearly wanted to join your fellow Americans for the rededication of the Statue of Liberty scheduled for July 4 of this year. So when you finally arrived in the dead of night there was no doubt that Edward Field Winthrop had joined our ranks!

No sooner had you been sponged and footprinted than the shabby green delivery room at New York Hospital was filled with your lusty cries, and as soon as you were introduced to your parents everyone in the room knew that you had made a statement by your very size alone.

While your mother was taken to the recovery room, I was allowed to spend twenty minutes with you alone in the labor room. After a very long day dealing with doctors and nurses with your mother in discomfort, I can only describe those moments with you as sublime. You cried for very little. When you did I was able to rock you into a peaceful trance. When I began talking to you, you gave me a very visible yawn. Since you are clearly going to have a mind of your own with interests of your own, I suspect this will not be the first yawn aimed at your father, who sometimes makes unnecessary comments or even speeches.

But before I released you back to the nurses, aware as I have been three times before of the miracle of human creation, I wanted to tell you about your name...

We had a very difficult time deciding what kind of a name to give you. Benjamin, Charles, and Harry were among the front-runners, but there were many more. Finally, we settled on Edward Field, your maternal grandfather and great grandfather's name. Both were men of distinction and character. Your great grandfather on your mother's side went west to St. Louis and helped open up the Mississippi to barge traffic. He was a pioneer in business and in spirit. His son, your grandfather, carried that tradition proudly. You will hear plenty about the Winthrop part of your heritage later on, but your mother and I wanted you to have a clear sense of identity. Even more importantly, we want you to know in this, the first day of your life, that both of us are crazy about you.

With love,
Dad

12

July 1986

Dear Ted,

As you grow up, let sports play an important part in your life. It doesn't make any difference which sport. One doesn't have to be a great athlete to benefit from the exercise and sociability sports can bring.

If you have the interest, try to enjoy sports as a spectator as well and to back a team. Baseball is our national sport. It captivates and fascinates many spectators every year. Since the age of four your Dad grew to enjoy playing this game. Shortly thereafter I began watching games. Since I was born in Boston and spent my boyhood near Boston, there was no question about which team was my team: the Boston Red Sox.

Although the Braves were also in Boston during the decade of the 1940's, the Red Sox had the magic, and if a young boy could love a team, this kid certainly loved the Red Sox. I still do.

The legendary Babe Ruth began his career with the Bosox, but by the 1940's the home team was cultivating such unforgettable heroes as Johnny Pesky, Bobby Doerr and Dominick DiMaggio (better than his brother Joe). Ted Williams was making baseball history and giving the crowds a thrill with his towering blasts into right field. There was only one trouble. The Red Sox never produced a championship team.

They came close in 1946 against the St. Louis Cardinals but lost in the final game of the World Series. In fact, upon studying all the record books I learned that the Boston Red Sox had not won a World Series since 1918. They still haven't won a World Series in my lifetime!

If you develop a love affair with a team as I have, dear son, you will find that it is very, very painful when your team loses. Maybe you will want to select a team that wins more frequently than the Sox have in my lifetime. Every year over nearly half a century I have followed the progress of my team. Moments of greatest pain came when the Sox lost to the rival Yankees. My New York friends, knowing of my addiction, had a great time every time their team beat mine – which was more frequently than the other way around.

Having seen the Red Sox come close to playing championship ball in the 1970's hasn't made up for all the discomfort – but I still believe life is richer with sports and with a favorite team being a part of the entire experience.

This year the Red Sox have had a stronger year than usual with stronger pitching coming from new talent, Boyd and Clements, and strong hitting from

Boggs, Rice, Baylor and others. In fact, the month you were born they were leading their division. I write this rather whimsical letter to you as my team looks forward to its first Series against the New York Yankees in 1986; I'm still hopeful despite the fact that my team has started strong in recent years and finished all too frequently near the middle of the pack or worse.

Who knows? This year it may be different. And, whatever happens, I look forward to taking you to a baseball game someday.

Love,
Dad

Dear Ted,

Today we had a nature walk. As soon as I arrived home from the office I picked you up and carried you outside. Your disposition improved immediately. As we walked around the house and into our little garden the air smelled of lilacs. In the late afternoon sunlight everything seemed to glow. The pinks and whites and reds and blues of the garden caught your attention as you glanced around. You even wanted to eat a flower after smelling it with me.

Each evening about this hour crows seem to gather for a party in the meadow. The noise this evening was particularly loud. Some mysterious conflict brought other participants, so that within minutes a variety of birds and several crows dominated the scene over the peaceful meadow.

Your attention span on this more distant action was short, however. Very abruptly a full grown rabbit leapt out of the bushes beneath our feet and hopped tamely in front of us no more than five yards away. Then he stopped to look at us out of the corner of his eye. You found this positively hilarious and broke out in a loud laughter. The bunny hopped. You laughed again. Three or four times this happened. Each time the furry bundle jumped you laughed. How I wish I had the entire episode on a video camera!

Then, in an experimental mood, I put you on the grass hoping you would crawl over to your new friend. No such luck! Rather than crawl toward the fearless rabbit, now located near some shrubbery, you reached for me to pick you up again.

We continued circling the house admiring the azaleas and the juniper bushes in the front of our house. We then wandered up to the side door, took a deep breath, and walked in.

The trip was a memorable one. We made an unspoken pact that we were outdoor lovers and confirmed environmentalists. We will make other trips like that one in the future, but I doubt we will be able to duplicate the encounter with the rabbit.

Love,
Dad

May 1987

Dear Ted,

Early this morning I heard you turn over in your crib and say something incomprehensible – the way you have so many other mornings in recent months. Getting up quietly from my bed and then tip-toeing into the hallway I quietly opened your door.

There you were facing the far wall of your crib crouching on all fours with your bottom wiggling, obviously in the early stages of awakening.

Within a few seconds you had maneuvered sideways in the crib. You glanced up and recognized a familiar shape in the doorway.

Suddenly you stood up and beamed – filling the darkened room with sunshine.

You reached into the air for me to pick you up. I did so and walked you down-stairs all sleepy-faced.

Love,
Dad

Dear Field,

Since your name is Edward Field Winthrop, I'll be calling you Field from time to time. Maybe it will stick. In fact Bayard, your brother, seems to be calling you Field quite regularly.

President Reagan is called "the great communicator" but over the past few weeks you have won my vote as the man most deserving of that title. Some examples...

During a recent trip to Charleston you communicated displeasure when we took you to a nice restaurant by kicking over your mother's soup. A few minutes later you were charming a gathering crowd outside the window by waving, banging on the window, and shrieking delight.

Each day in Charleston I would walk you through Charleston's back streets and along the waterfront by the Battery. There wasn't a cat or a dog, a horse or a bird that didn't receive greetings from you. You were also as friendly with total strangers as they were with us – far more so here than in New York!

Upon arriving in Greenwich your mother had to go to work on Tuesdays and Wednesdays. This means that for two days a week you are left with Cering – the most loving and thorough caregiver imaginable. Your mother's early morning departures also mean that I am left to say goodbye. Your communication of joy and wanting to play and explore with me are never stronger than in these moments before my own departure from home or after my arrival from work in the evening.

This morning you heard me on the other side of the door from your room. By the time I had quietly arrived at the other door to your room, your disappointment in not being able to reach the handle to the door was very evident, but as you turned around and saw me your face filled with happiness. You bolted toward my outstretched arms and joined me for a brief tour outside. Rocks, frogs and the birdhouse held your fascination. As always, this magic time together was cut short by my need to catch a train. As with your brothers before you I am finding once again that these quality moments in early childhood are all too brief. My sadness upon leaving is only partly relieved by writing you this letter.

Love,
Dad

September 1987

Dear Ted,

Years from now I want to recall in vivid detail the sight of you being released by Cering at the top of the stairs in our Greenwich home. Upon my exit from our room you filled my world with sunlight as you broke into a broad grin and raced toward me as fast as your little legs could carry you. In fact you ran so fast that you literally fell into my extended arms as you reached me.

But it is that brilliant smile that I want to carry everywhere with me. The thought that I could bring such joy to you fills me up with happiness. Your smile and your laughter fills every room with sunshine. You bring joy to everyone you meet, but the joy you bring to your mother and father is greater than you can ever imagine.

Part of this is because all expressions and emotions are so pure in the first two years of life. There is no veneer, no disguise, no dishonesty. Another part is that you have a wonderfully expressive face – filled with character and punctuated by sparkling, engaging light blue eyes. Your mother says you're perfect and she might just be right – at least for now!

With love,
Dad

Dear Ted,

Over Christmas and New Year's you have changed from a barrel of energy to a barrel of energy that speaks. If you can be categorized as an early walker you also may fairly be considered a late talker. So I was plenty happy to hear those first words arrive.

It's difficult to say which words are the first – for anyone, I guess – because words come out by accident sometimes. By now, however, we know that "Da" (Dad), "Mama," "Sa" (Cering), "Shnow" (Snow), Dog, Bye-bye, Night-night, and a few others are among your first words. You are beginning to communicate with your fellow man as we enter 1988.

Another observation worth passing on for the record is that you are curious about how things work. Clocks, lamps, radios and various other gadgets seem to hold your attention much better than the toys which have been sent to you by admirers for your amusement. It's not that you don't like toys, it's just that you seem to have an intense curiosity about how things work – a trait, I might add, that comes from your grandfather, Edward Field Goltra. Winthrops congratulate themselves when they figure out how to screw in a light bulb, so you might become the "fix it" man in the Winthrop family – if you don't destroy everything first.

The next two years are bound to be challenging ones for your parents. Your energy and your sense of curiosity are keeping us on our toes and promise to keep both of us and Cering very busy. Every day is proving to be an adventure with you around. I only wish you would appreciate the joys of sleeping through the night.

Love,
Dad

Dear Ted,

I often wonder about the fragile nature of the male ego. Somehow, I think, men are born with a higher sense of mission and a higher need to prove themselves. Perhaps this is the direct result of our not being able to have babies. We can't seem to prove ourselves or to fulfill ourselves as obviously as women.

This sensitive subject is often highlighted by the first born, or the only child. We are more driven, more achievement-oriented than other siblings. Perhaps we are less relaxed and less happy as well. Surely this point was made by the studies made of the applicants for the astronaut program years ago. Most of these candidates were the first born or the only sons in their families.

It may be that these half-baked theories hold no water, but it does seem more than just coincidence that you and Jay and I may be the most achievement-oriented of our sibling groups. We also may be the most high strung and the most energized.

Love,
Dad

Dear Ted,

You will understand as well as any of us the importance of dreams. Roots and wings – or a sense of the past and hopes for the future – these are the most important gifts that can be passed from one generation to the next, in my view.

But back to dreams...there have been times when all our dreams for the future seem unachievable. For you it might be reaching the ranks of a professional athlete or returning to the joys of a home on Groton Plantation. For me it was at one time repairing the effects of a broken marriage or building a plantation on Ivanhoe. I have had dreams about my firm, about your future, about my brother or my sister – all of them with happy endings.

Whether or not these and other dreams are grounded in reality, it has become increasingly more obvious to me that it is dreams that sustain us through difficult times. In this sense dreams for the future have a powerful, positive effect.

In fact, it might make sense to take a collection of these letters to you and make them into a book. How's that for a dream? The book wouldn't sell much, though – no sex or violence contained therein!

Love,
Dad

March 1988

Dear Ted,

All my life – or at least all my adult life – I have been blessed with good health. For the past twenty-five years I have never missed a day of work because of poor health. This is not likely to go on much longer, but while I am relatively well, I would like to pause a moment with you and count my blessings.

As a young man I was never a champion of parties or of beer consumption. Nor was I the health freak your older brothers might claim to be from time to time. Rather, I cut a path along the middle of the road – smoking for a few years, drinking to excess occasionally, competing in sports and trying half-heartedly to keep in shape.

Now in mid-life, I realize that good health is appreciated far more when the threat of sickness can be seen at close quarters. Some friends have passed away; others have lost their vitality through illness. When I think about the good fortune I have experienced through the years – good health, wonderful children, reasonably good luck in my work bringing me enjoyment and opportunity, I can easily claim Thanksgiving as my favorite holiday.

Love,
Dad

Dear Teddie,

Intelligent people have suggested that it is irresponsible to produce children with all the problems the world faces today. The environmental problems seem overwhelming. The depletion of the ozone layer, the reduction of vegetation and pure water, and the threat of wildlife extinction point toward life becoming more difficult for all of us in the years ahead.

The economy too is fragile. Global debt constitutes a cloud hanging over our banking system; consumer debt indicates that we are a nation of champion consumers – not savers; the national debt has reached frightening proportions, alerting us that the next recession may be worse than unpleasant.

In the arena of nuclear weapons and military hardware mankind has found it difficult – if not impossible – to reduce the risks of global catastrophe. The concept of the interdependency and brotherhood of nations seems, at times, to have escaped global consciousness. Small wars persist and the nuclear giants are only beginning to address the problem in a serious manner.

And yet your mother and I decided quite consciously to have you, our child. Why? Perhaps it was a leap of faith, perhaps it was the life force Bernard Shaw talked about, perhaps it was the egotistical notion that a combination of both of us would constitute a pretty special person. Most likely it was all of the above.

Whatever the outcome, ultimately you should know that you have brought the two of us enormous joy and satisfaction over the first twenty-two months of your life. More than that you have given us future orientation. You have kept us awake nearly every night but you make us laugh. You destroy our home routinely but you make us proud. You have given us physical bruises and childhood bugs but we have never felt healthier.

Without sounding dramatic or claiming originality it can be said that your generation gives hope for the future. I have become a believer!

Love,
Dad

Dear Ted,

It looks as if I won't be pushing you around in a carriage much more. Five months ago your mother and I moved to Charleston to establish a new life in a wonderful city. Your mother had worked in Washington and in New York; I had come from Boston and put in my time on Wall Street. Together we decided to move to Charleston.

Today I had planned to push you through the historic district to smell the sweet air of early morning, to listen to the birds and to contemplate all the reasons we moved to Charleston. My plan was to go home and write you this note – one in a series of letters I am writing to you on the theory that one day you may want to see how your father dreamed and theorized on all kinds of subjects.

Our ride broke up on King Street, however, as you absolutely refused to be pushed in the carriage. Now at younger than two you can become a tightly wound twenty-five-pound bundle of energy hurling defiance in all directions – particularly for an audience and particularly if you want to see fire trucks! Passersby must have been amused seeing your father in a business suit trying to keep you in the carriage looking as if he had sprinted two hundred yards and was completely worn out by the process.

Still it seems worth reflecting on why your mother and I chose Charleston above all other places to live in America. Now that I have recovered from that rather public scene with you, the reflection seems worth the effort.

Firstly, Charleston allows the visitor or the inhabitant to appreciate history in the broadest sense. With all the grace and elegance of the buildings having been preserved with care, people here have respect for history in their bones. If it didn't exist a few decades ago, it certainly exists now. The city has been managed well with a high level of regard for preserving the architectural and historic integrity of the place.

Charleston, Philadelphia and Boston were once the largest cities in America; now Charleston alone among them offers the opportunity to stroll down narrow streets and observe the surroundings remotely similar to the scene one or two centuries ago.

In addition, the environmental condition of the city has been respected. Birds of many species dart in and out of trees and back yards across the historic district; Battery Park offers a commanding view of the water; the parks offer quiet places to rest and think. All of these virtues were important to me, because I was brought up on the coast of Massachusetts with frequent vacations in the woods of South Carolina where wildlife abounds and where, as a young boy, I had heard about Charleston.

Your mother likes urban life and, more than any other city we could find, Charleston offered the advantages of a city with those of the great outdoors. Your mother particularly enjoys many of the small shops and fine restaurants.

Perhaps as important, the city appeared to offer cultural attractions and an intellectual fabric which we hope will provide you with all the key elements of a good education.

Finally, the people are warm and friendly – allowing even the new-comer to establish roots and feel a part of the community. It could be said that Charleston offered roots to the past as well as hope and opportunity, or wings for the future. If parents can offer their child roots and wings and a good education, that covers a good deal of our agenda.

So as you hurl yourself out of the baby carriage next time, or cry about wanting to go and see the fire engines in the Meeting Street fire house, please consider the needs of your father to observe and contemplate. And please don't try to dive out of your carriage. That wears me out.

With love,
Dad

May 1988

Dear Teddie,

It is my hope that you will want to grow trees. But you, my youngest son, are under two years old, and I am beyond the half century mark in age, so our perspectives may be a little different.

Yesterday I held you up to the branch of a small tree in our Charleston garden. You held on to it with the enthusiasm of a monkey. I found you had the strength to hang from it for a surprisingly long time. Then once your little arms had stopped aching you called out "tree-tree" again and again. Clearly you wanted to hang from a tree and perhaps to climb among its branches. That activity will start in earnest within a few days.

But trees are good for more than climbing. They cleanse the air; they offer protection and homes for wildlife and birds; they reduce wind and soil erosion. In addition they add beauty and quality to our lives. Growing trees can even be a good business.

Years ago I purchased some land in the southern part of South Carolina. While there were trees and green fields on it, the property had not been actively managed for a while. As a businessman and as an environmentalist, I was determined to preserve the environmental beauty of the property while, at the same time, creating a company with diversified sources of income and financial stability.

Our first move was to drain nearly half the land by creating a ditch which, in turn, fed into a creek. The creek became a scenic pond almost immediately with the benefit of a new and steady water supply. A dam was built to create a boundary and shoreline. Trees on the other end of the small plantation were made accessible by the drainage of the ditch. Once dry, selective cutting began with a clear view of planting many small seedlings.

Open fields that were not planted provided good grazing area for deer; quail could often be found on the edges and throughout the woods. Quail and deer hunting rights constituted a second source of income after trees. In time a pattern of profitability, improvement of wildlife habitat, and the planting of trees annually was established. After several years a cabin was built on the property, which had been incorporated. This cabin would in turn be rented, constituting a third primary source of income.

Perhaps the greatest satisfaction has come from the psychic dividends or the enjoyment of being there – of seeing wood ducks nest in the boxes we placed around the forty-acre pond, of listening to the floodtide of wildlife sounds on the steps of our cabin at dusk or in the early morning. Unexpectedly, we have also found ancient Indian artifacts of some significance on the property. Pottery, arrowheads and the camping grounds will be inspected by a qualified archaeologist from the University of South Carolina this summer.

But without question the element that has given our hideaway its character is the trees. Slash and loblolly and long leaf pine, cypress and oak and beech and holly and many other species of trees have provided all the benefits outlined above. There are more trees on the property today, with a greater diversity of species, than when we became owners. And yet, with careful and selective cutting, we have generated enough income to cover our cost of the property twenty-five years ago and pay for a couple of cabins as well.

Maybe you can understand better why I was so pleased to see you warm up to the tree in our backyard.

Soon we will try to plant a few trees together. Hopefully that will give pleasure to others long after we're gone.

With love,
Dad

Dear Teddie:

There are a number of times when you seem older than you are:

- When you put on your fireman's hat – often at a racy tilt over one eye.
- When you say "Oh no" after spilling something.
- When you walk upstairs or downstairs taking one step at a time – just like an adult.
- When you jump into the driver's seat of my car, take the wheel – and then, almost as an afterthought, place a tape in the automobile's tape deck.
- When you take off most of your clothes in preparation for a bath.
- When you walk outside the front door and then down the street without even looking over your shoulder.
- When you reach for a glass of bourbon and slug it down with more enthusiasm than I can muster.
- When you stroll with your hands clasped behind you in the fashion of Prince Charles or some other member of royalty.
- When you go up to a small person and give him or her an accepting and warm hug.
- When you run with vigor pumping your arms like an athlete.

All of these mannerisms and gestures leave us amused – and even more aware – of how rapidly you are growing up, although not yet two years old.

But then you reverse the impressions – by becoming shy, by clinging dependently to either parent, or by crying in despair; then we know we will have you as an infant son for many more months.

With love,
Dad

June 1988

Dear Ted,

Over the past year we have spent a good deal of time in Charleston, South Carolina – a town much closer in spirit and tempo to Boston, where I grew up, than to Greenwich. Returning to Greenwich after seven months away may leave each of us with differing impressions. As an active two-year-old you have not given me your impressions of this community but I thought I might try to share mine with you...

Greenwich has changed more than most big towns during this brief blink of time. While I always knew that it was a fluid society with changes occurring continually, it is striking the number of new houses being built (and not necessarily sold). The number of new stores in place and the number of cars lined up during the rush hour make an impression as well.

These are hip shot impressions from a modern-day Rip Van Winkle who has returned after only these few months away. But it is clear that the pace of change in Greenwich is far more rapid than in Charleston. People come and go faster; move faster; change jobs faster. The roots are not so deep and the effects of nearby New York are far greater than anything influencing most other communities. Friendships and commitments seem different here – although value judgements are dangerous. The pace of life and the pace of change are very rapid. There is no mistake about that.

As an environmental nut I cannot resist making a few passing observations. With more traffic and more building the air seems more full of a barely perceptible grey pollution than before. Maybe it's the summer heat, but the visibility has deteriorated.

The trip on the ferry boat to the island is still great fun, but with the paper full of reports on the quality of life at the beaches, one notices that the sea water is less than pure – perhaps no worse than last summer, but certainly no better.

As for the roads – both within town and out in the back country – there is more traffic than a year or two ago. One has to start the day earlier if he or she wants an unhampered trip to the train station or a parking space without problems.

Having said all of the above it is wonderful seeing you return to the land of your birth. You are in your bones a creature of the northeast. Your limited vocabulary shows no trace of a southern accent.

Despite the pollution, despite the noise and the pace of life in Connecticut, it

29

seems to agree with you. You run with even more intensity. You smell the flowers and marvel at the bunnies in the open fields. You love the cars in motion, the boats in motion and the people in motion.

Your friends Frazer, Mark and Elizabeth are back in Charleston where the flowers bloom and people have better manners. But you will make new friends in both places who will bring you as much pleasure in the future as our friends bring us today as we return after months away.

Your capacity for adapting to change continues to amaze your parents and you don't have to look very hard to find flowers that bloom and people that smile here in Greenwich as well as in Charleston.

Love,
Dad

Dear Ted,

A terrible thing happened as you reached out of the car window for me, when I returned from a trip last week. I slammed the back door of the car, not realizing your little arm extended into the path of the closing door.

Instantly I reached for you and carried you away from the car where your mother sat helplessly. Both of us were tormented by the idea that your wrist or arm may have been broken by the impact.

Immediately we took you to the fire house, glancing at your arm with the diagonal bruise on it. By the time we arrived at the fire house, however, we knew you would be OK. Your mind was on the fire trucks and you had no trouble climbing vigorously aboard as we walked you over to the largest one of all accompanied by a fireman for the first time.

What a tough little nut your are! It's a pleasure to share your company.

Love,
Dad

Dear Ted,

There are a number of thoughts I would like to share with you as you get a little older. Although I know things will change drastically in another decade or so, we'll be discussing weighty matters such as the following:

- We are moving rapidly toward a global society; the world has shrunk a great deal since my time in college. All you can learn about other cultures and about how people can better communicate during these complicated times will be important.

- The computer is king. It is important to understand its uses and applications in your work. I have not learned computer disciplines but want to encourage you to understand how these marvelous machines work.

- As for your major field of concentration in your studies, I would encourage you to get the basic liberal arts disciplines under your belt – English, history philosophy, government, art, music – these are the fields of study which have distinguished and identified civilized men, in my opinion, and made their lives richer. Business, the law, and further specialization can wait.

- Reach for the best teachers among the professors. One of the most interesting and memorable courses I took as a freshman was Music I – simply because that subject was taught by a marvelous man who introduced me to the great composers, just as the world of Chaucer and the great artists were opened up to me by outstanding men.

- In addition to all of the above you will have an opportunity to develop your spiritual being. Understand that your Episcopalian heritage is a key part of your foundation. I hope you will become a member of an Episcopal church and that you will consider getting confirmed someday, and getting married in a church eventually.

- Sports will remain a part your life, I hope, since all other aspects of your life – including your opinion of yourself – are invariably bound with your physical health and vitality.

- Perhaps most importantly, cultivate high quality friends and have a grand time with them. The adventure ahead of you is bound to be a rich one, wherever it leads, and it is your friends that will give all of it real meaning.

This is all a bit premature since you are only two years old, but I thought you should have my thoughts for the record when you get older and when you can digest it.

Love,
Dad

December 1988

Dear Teddie,

This letter is about your mother in particular, and all women in general. As you may have discovered, your mother is a very competent woman. While her energy level may not be as high as yours or mine, her use of energy and common sense has won her praise in three different careers – in the White House under two Republican presidents, on Wall Street in two different firms and at Time, Inc. under several administrations. (Meanwhile I have had a hard enough time struggling with one career!) Your mother never took on a stint with the Peace Corps ("the toughest job you'll ever love"), but it seems she has done quite a few other things, including volunteer work from time to time and working in a shoe store.

There is no question in my mind, however, that the most satisfying job your mother took on is that of being a mother. To date she has received no pay and very little gratitude for this work. The hours are terrible; she gets between four and six hours of sleep every night. The fringe benefits, such as medical help and vacations and pensions are not terrific either; in fact she has given these up.

But the reward of hearing you call "Mommy" makes up for everything. When you get a little older I hope you and I can toast your mother with a glass of wine – and while we're at it, perhaps we can toast all mothers everywhere.

Love,
Dad

January 1989

Dear Ted,

You seem to love walking outside with me in Ivanhoe. Maybe you are aware that the walk around the pond is my favorite place in the world at this point in my life. Or perhaps in some instinctive way, you realize that your mother is developing thoughts on creating a dock and garden area complete with lights and bushes in this very special place.

In any event you take me by the hand and lead me to sticks. Whacking the sticks against trees or throwing them into the water ranks high on your list of kicks these days...and I don't mind it either. Besides, I'm pretty good at generating splintered wood or creating a splash when I have such an appreciative partner by my side.

Ivanhoe is our retreat in the wilderness. It's next to Groton Plantation, which is more than ten times as big and owned by more than ten of us. But Ivanhoe belongs to us. It is being built by us, developed by us, and most of all, protected by us for future family and friends to enjoy.

Today Ivanhoe consists of 1,423 acres of fields and trees. While we are protecting stands of sawtimber for the future, we are also growing many rows of small pine – mostly slash and loblolly. Since the beginning we have put roughly a million trees in the ground, I would guess. Only a few of these will reach full maturity – after we have gone – but a beginning has been made in creating a retreat for the family which also is dedicated to the wisdom of growing trees.

My hope, of course, is that you and your brothers will carry on this exercise. Meanwhile, we will have some fun in roaming along the shore, discovering sticks that need to be broken or tossed in the water, or even taking a ride in a boat under the towering cypress trees.

With love,
Dad

January 1989

Dear Ted,

It seemed a long ways from Greenwich this past weekend. We went for a ride in our canoe on the pond of our tree farm near the Savannah River. Let me describe the experience before closing with a message.

Nearly all my desk work had been cleared up in Charleston. Your mother and I packed our bags in preparation for the one-hundred-mile drive to our retreat in the Southern part of the state.

All of my adult life I had been planting trees on this property and developing it in a way that preserved its environmental integrity. At the same time, I have done my very best to keep a positive flow of income from the property and preserve a strong balance sheet.

In addition to finding ancient Indian relics of the Yuchee tribe on the property, we have recently built two cabins near a long forty-acre pond which constitutes a border of the property. The psychic dividends have been beyond expectation.

At the wonderful age of two, you are already appreciating the natural wonders of our place, which we call Ivanhoe. As we turned off the road late in the afternoon, you began to ask about whether or not we would see any owls. You imitated their call perfectly. Your eyes lit up as we drove alongside a field. You hoped we would see some deer.

When we arrived at the larger cabin with its glass front facing the pond, you didn't bother to linger over its Adirondack-style porch, or to admire the timber peg interior, or even to play with some toys you left behind last time. Rather, you ran straight to the edge of that wondrous pond alongside two canoes which had been pulled up on the shore.

Directly ahead of us, tall cypress trees grow out of the pond's depths. The glassy pond extends in both directions under these majestic trees. The air is pure – no bugs at this time of year. A slight breeze was coming in off the water and whispered through the loblolly pines alongside us.

Up on one side, some wood ducks had already spotted us and were screeching their alarm as they climbed out of the water and flew skyward. The air smelled of pine needles.

As always, I wanted to drink in all this scenery before doing anything; to settle back into the rocker on the porch in hopes of seeing a beaver or a bobcat, an otter or a turtle. But you had other plans. You climbed into one of the canoes and ordered me to get a paddle and a life jacket. I complied.

After some effort, we pulled the boat into the water. Rather than put you up front, the way I will in a few short years, I put you firmly between my knees in the middle of the boat. I was to do the paddling; your mother was to oversee the operation quietly from the safety of the shore. She remained terrified that one of the alligators would take you away as an appetizer before his dinner.

In this way, one of life's great adventures began for both of us. You remained quiet, sensing the canoe was tipsy and dangerous. I paddled noiselessly – gliding swiftly under the trees and through the water. The purity of this experience, the peace of the undisturbed wilderness will remain with me – and perhaps both of us – for a long, long time.

Some fish surfaced, and birds calling broke the silence under the darkening sky – but the dominating feeling was one of peace and tranquility. It was indeed a long way from Greenwich or even Charleston, South Carolina. It is important that we try to go on a canoe trip many times in the future.

Pulling the canoe up on the bank once our adventure was over, it occurred to me that we were no more than a few miles from the Savannah River Plant, recently in the newspapers as a symbol of environmental ruin and government waste. Hydrogen bombs are built there; huge sums of government funds are spent there. DuPont and the Department of Energy were supposed to protect all of us from careless errors, but the reality is that there were a number of unreported mishaps over the last few decades since the 1950's. The newspapers have been tracking the controversy for several months now.

Regretfully, there has not been enough citizen involvement in protecting the environment nationwide and worldwide. Many naively assume that our interests will be protected and the environment will be preserved by those "wisely" governing us. In years past, these assumptions have not been entirely valid. Perhaps if more of us had been more fortunate in getting out into the wilderness this way with our children, we would have been more involved in the process. We would have learned the absolute necessity of protecting our fragile ecosystem.

As you grow older, Teddie, there will be no alternative. All of us will have to be involved in this effort, because options have begun to close in on us. The greenhouse effect, which we read about, is only one of the problems facing us. Forests are being destroyed; endangered species are dying out; pure water is being contaminated; the effects of acid rain are multiplying. The list goes on and on.

It seemed terribly important, after this splendid experience in the canoe, to commit this thought to writing in hopes that you will have the chance to go for a trip with your child in a canoe some day.

Love,
Dad

February 1989

Dear Ted,

Getting back to that walk along the shore of Ivanhoe, I want to remember the way in which you shape phrases and sentences during these months. As we walked toward the water you reached for a stick, slapped it in the water, and then asked, "Is the water for the boats?"... rather than "are boats for the water?"

Similarly in the early blackness or dusty gray of 5:00 a.m., you have been known to say "it's getting morning."

Few things give you greater pleasure these days than Daddy's "glubbs" (gloves), or in wearing shoes or boots that are far too big for you. Some say such antics are a bit odd, but they seem to be your trademark.

At Groton Plantation you also enjoy hearing the dogs "woofing," patting the horses' noses – or even sticking your finger up their nostril. You also seem enthralled by chasing bugs. If you're not an animal lover yet you certainly enjoy their company. You were very upset by being unable to catch a lizard on the Ivanhoe porch before we left.

Speaking of likes and preferences, you certainly seemed to appreciate each of your older half-brothers when they arrived, in turn, at our Charleston home over the holiday season.

You remembered them without a doubt as you dragged them around the house to show off your toys, your room or any object which caught your fancy. Needless to say this brought me great pleasure as did all of the above.

Love,
Dad

February 1989

Dear Ted,

You and I went to church last Sunday. We went to a different kind of church –
all black, all Baptist, and in the rural part of South Carolina. It was a small
church I had been involved in repairing some years ago, as an outsider who
wanted to fulfill a promise to an old man in the community.

We arrived early at Bethlehem Church and parked outside on the sandy sur-
face, dwarfed by the towering pine trees all around us. The February air was
cold and damp as we made our way into the freshly painted white structure
with green trim.

The service began with the most marvelous spiritual. Frank Brown, an old
friend with a wide generous face and a sunburst of a smile, was dressed in a
well-tailored suit for the first time since I had known him. The rest of the time
he had always been in work clothes carrying wood or working around the
kitchen. Frank opened the service with a low, vibrant baritone that began in his
toes and ankles and filled the Church. His marvelous voice dominated the
choir and led the congregation. The rest of those present followed in joyful
syncopated rhythm – no organ, not even a piano.

Toward the end, the preacher welcomed us into the Church – knowing perhaps
that I had a certain history and involvement with the place. I could only express
my gratitude for being included and my sense of appreciation for the music.

It was indeed a wonderful occasion which ended shortly after you toppled off
the church bench, banging your head on the hard wood. Your ear turned scar-
let, but the interruption to the service was minimal. Miraculously you seemed to
understand the need to be quiet. Without a doubt, however, the morning had
been a rich one for all of us – a new kind of adventure, yes, but far more than
that. The extent to which this small group (less than thirty in all) felt close to
God – the one created by a white society, after all, was impressive; the intensity of the service made a real impression; the music was unforgettable. I con-
cluded that it was difficult to feel more connected than this.

Yet when we departed and expressed our appreciation once again, I could
only think how far away all of this seemed from the world we knew. And then I
found myself hoping we would return again some day together when you would
be able to remember and appreciate more of what happened.

Love,
Dad

Dear Ted,

Now that you are approaching three years old, you seem to be learning that a high degree of skepticism is a good thing. You seem to be very careful as you climb the steps to the top of the slide in the playground. Likewise, you step gingerly into my canoe as we prepare to glide through the swamp waters of our pond here in South Carolina. Finally, you do not always eat something you are told to eat just because you are told it tastes good.

All of these are healthy signs, I believe. It is far better to discover things on our own. One bad fall or misstep can be a positive experience. Furthermore, those who would lead us are not always "on the side of the angels." If you think about it, some of the great tidal moves in American society in recent years have not been initiated by our enlightened leaders but rather by ordinary citizens like you and me who had the fortitude to speak out. The civil rights movement, the end of the Vietnam War and the women's movement are only three easy examples of how skepticism, combined with a constructive sense of initiating a change of direction, has paid off.

Let me carry this line of reasoning a step further. Many professions demonstrate a protective shield which almost says to the outside world, "we are the only ones who truly understand the complexities of our profession; therefore stand back and accept what we say as Gospel."

Whoever invented the idea that war was too important to be left up to the generals should be blessed. The same accusation should be aimed at other professions as well, in my view. Lawyers seem to get so wrapped up in their trade that any similarity between true justice and that which emerges from the courts is purely coincidental. Be skeptical of that which motivates many people.

In medicine I have seen examples where sick people were kept alive with terribly sophisticated machinery without any regard for the dignity of dying or the feelings of the family. Someone once said that more people make a living out of cancer than die from it. I can believe it. In any case laymen are not encouraged to venture onto the elevated turf of doctors and make judgements or frequently it appears that way. Again I would say, "be skeptical."

In my own profession of asset management these truths are most clearly evident as well. We go to business school; we are encouraged to believe that we know how to analyze an ongoing business or a good investment. Yet look at the so-called professionals, the high-powered, well-educated, institutional money managers who compete with one another in managing mutual funds and other huge pools of money. Most of them have been unable to beat the Dow Jones Industrial Average over the past five years. And yet we posture as professionals, insulted all too often if our moves are questioned by "outsiders.' It is a curious fact that Warren Buffet, one of the most successful money managers, has operated out of Omaha, Nebraska, not Wall Street, throughout much of his professional life. Humility is very much a part of his style. Be skeptical of the so-called pros. The best in any profession are all too aware of their frailties.

Be skeptical also of our government leaders who assume the role of protecting our environment. Now we live close to the Savannah River Plant in Aiken, South Carolina. The Government has been less than direct about how our interests have been protected by those in charge. Your mother and I went to listen to Frances Hart last week here in Charleston. We learned about the unbelievable damage that might be done by those in charge of this plant which has been used to create tritium for nuclear warheads in recent years. We were told that the clean up work required at this stage exceeds $100 million. Clearly the world does not need more weapons of destruction today.

Indeed it is clear that intelligent citizens must stand up and speak out on this matter. For too many years too many of us have passively sat back and allowed this and other facilities to produce material which destroys the fragile environment of this planet on which we live. Be skeptical of those who govern.

Those of us in my generation have been far too silent for far too long. Let me make up for it in part by urging you and your fine brothers to speak out on matters where you have a clear conviction. Use your clear minds, continue to take measured steps on your way up to the top of the slide, but reject something you are told is good for you until you discover for yourself!

Love,
Dad

July 1989

Dear Ted,

Now that you are three years old and seem to enjoy putting coins in your mouth, it seems appropriate to add to my series of letters to you with a few of my viewpoints on the complicated subject of money. I recall your grandfather's words to me when I was a small boy: "You better be careful if you're born with a silver spoon in your mouth, because you might choke on it!"

Even at the age of three you have learned that the penny you carried in your mouth for a hundred yard sprint nearly a year ago can be a force for good and for bad. When you swallowed it you and I experienced an event neither of us will forget easily. Fortunately you survived the experience! You have also learned that it takes more than one or two coins to get a wad of bubble gum (your first choice) or a present for your mother (the better choice).

In a somewhat deeper sense you will learn that money can evolve as a formidable force for good or evil in your life. It doesn't take your father or an investment advisor to instruct you in the various ways money can be used in a destructive way to control the actions of others.

This behavior can take subtle and not so subtle forms. If a parent suggests that he or she will give money only if the child conforms to certain expectations, such a threat rarely has a positive effect. (I promise to make a big effort not to do this with you, because I believe your behavior can be shaped in other ways.) If a public official accepts a bribe in the placing of a lucrative contract, this, too, is an evil use of money. It can be punished in a court of law.

More frequently, money seems to be divisive among families, giving rise to jealousy, anger and public battles. Over the years I have seen this happen too many times among families having more than an average share of financial resources.

Needless to say, there are many ways wealth has been used as a force for good. Our community offers many cases worth mentioning, but a couple of examples will suffice. Several years ago a Greenwich family was involved in a capital drive for a worthy cause. Anxious to create a vehicle for charitable giving, a private foundation was created to fund future gifts out of the income stream. Now that the original pledge has been satisfied, the family has established a pool of assets, the income of which is distributed among a wide variety of educational and environmental organizations. The enjoyment and satisfaction this has brought to the family members who are involved has energized everyone – donor and donees alike!

Many more examples can be given: individuals banding together to create many funds benefiting a community, as in Community Trust of New York and similar organizations in other areas. Some people, recognizing the fact that they have been beneficiaries of the free enterprise system, have created stand-alone charitable trusts dedicated to helping the less fortunate. Frequently these charitable trusts or foundations are perpetual in nature, distributing only the income. But in all cases money is used as a positive, constructive force.

It is sometimes said that giving to charity is essentially selfish, bringing a joy to those involved in the process. Those who give to the United Way here in Greenwich or to a thousand other charities have experienced this kick from helping the community which helps all of us. Those who arrive in any community and leave without leaving anything behind are the losers.

Inherited money too often generates a feeling of guilt. Somehow the money doesn't seem to be one's own without the effort involved in making it. The businessman/capitalist wants to create a dynasty; the next generation ruins the plan by choking on guilt, the familiar silver spoon. This does not always happen, but it happens often enough to be worth mentioning. The only way out of this trap, it seems to me, is to give away all you inherit – to your children, to charities, to friends. Do it gradually, not impulsively; making money on your own will prove your self worth if it is necessary. Once everything is given away over a period of time you will have your own brand of freedom and a peaceful sense of inner pride.

This concludes my thoughts on a series of randomly selected subjects. Some of these letters have been whimsical, some serious, some humorous, but, as I should have said some time ago, none of them should be taken too seriously. All the things you learn on your own are best. But, as you might guess from the letters I have written to you in this book, I was inspired by a few of the things my father told me long ago.

With love,
Dad

www.ingramcontent.com/pod-product-compliance
Lightning Source LLC
Chambersburg PA
CBHW070829100426
42813CB00003B/551